MEN-AT-ARMS SERIES

EDITOR: MARTIN WINDROW
ALBAN BOOK SERVICES

Medieval European Armies

Text by TERENCE WISE
Colour plates by GERALD EMBLETON

OSPREY PUBLISHING LIMITED

Published in 1975 by
Osprey Publishing Ltd
59 Grosvenor Street, London W1X 9DA
© Copyright 1975 Osprey Publishing Ltd
Reprinted 1979, 1981, 1982, 1983, 1984, 1985, 1986,
1987, 1988 (twice)

Most of the black and white illustrations have been
taken from *A Critical Enquiry into Ancient Armour in
Europe*, vols. 1 and 2, by Sir Samuel Meyrick (1824)
and *A Treatise on Ancient Armour and Weapons* by
Francis Grose (1786). The photographs are repro-
duced by courtesy of the Keeper, the Library of the
Victoria and Albert Museum. (Photographer,
Berkhamsted Photographic, Berkhamsted, Hertford-
shire.) Sir Samuel Meyrick was the father of the study
of armour in England, and the first collector on an
extensive scale: much of his collection is now in the
Wallace Collection. The paintings in his book were
based on actual weapons and armour, or the evidence
supplied by tomb effigies, monuments and illuminated
manuscripts. The author and publisher wish to thank
the Royal Artillery Institution and the Wallace
Collection for supplying the remainder of the
photographs.

ISBN 0 85045 245 7

Filmset by BAS Printers Limited, Over Wallop,
Hampshire
Printed in Hong Kong

Introduction

Almost continual warfare raged in Europe during the period 1300–1500: the Hundred Years War between France and England; the Scottish wars and Wars of the Roses in England itself; the struggles for political and religious freedom from feudal overlords in Switzerland, Bohemia and Flanders; to stem the advance of the Turks in Hungary; between the city states, republics and papal territories of Italy; civil wars and the fight against the Moors in Spain; and the invasions of Italy by the French at the end of the 15th century. These wars were the furnaces in which many of the modern European nations were forged. Parallel with this emergence of the nations came the development of national armies to protect the newly-won borders and independence, yet throughout this period the old feudal method of raising an army persisted.

Raising a Feudal Army

Under the feudal system all land within a kingdom was owned by the king. He retained large estates to provide himself with personal followers and royal revenues, but the greater part of the kingdom was let in large lordships to his principal nobles on condition they maintained a certain number of men for the defence of the kingdom. These chief tenants of the Crown retained a portion of their land and sub-let the remainder in estates on condition that each noble or knight who held an estate supplied a proportion of the armed force required of the chief tenant by the king. A few of the chief tenants, particularly churchmen and German barons, preferred to maintain personal control over all their lands, supplying their quota of knights by hiring them,

these men being known as household knights. Each sub-tenant let the farms on his manor to copyholders on condition they provided themselves with the appropriate arms and mustered under his banner when called upon for military service. Therefore, each manor supplied a troop of soldiers, known as a retinue: the small farmers and the knight's personal retainers fighting on foot, clad in leather jerkins and armed with spear or bow, with perhaps two or three of his more important copyholders in padded and quilted body-armour and steel helmets; his younger brothers or sons as men-at-arms and squires on horseback with lance, sword and shield and in armour almost complete as his own; and the knight himself, fully armoured, armed with lance, sword and shield, and mounted on a heavy charger. (In the mid-fourteenth century the

A knight of the first half of the fourteenth century wearing some form of padded garment, possibly leather, over his hauberk and his mail hose reinforced by poleyns

Spearman with round shield and kettle hat and wearing scale armour, which was lighter and more flexible than mail and remained in service amongst infantrymen until c. 1325. Man-at-arms c. 1300 wearing hauberk (artists used a number of such methods to represent mail), mail hose and iron poleyns to protect his knees. Slinger of the early fourteenth century, completely unarmoured and carrying a staff sling for large missiles. The ordinary sling had a range of about 275 yards.

Longbowman in hauberk, hardened leather breastplate reinforced by four iron discs, and simple cervelliere helmet of the early fourteenth century. Note he is holding an arrow headed with a phial of quicklime. Extreme range was 300 yards, effective range about 200 yards. Crossbowman wearing helmet with nasal bar, also early fourteenth century, and carrying a short sword or possibly long dagger. Ranges were about the same as the longbow but the crossbow was much slower to load and lacked the penetrative power of the longbow

retinue of Richard Lord Talbot was 14 knights, 60 squires and 82 archers; that of John de Vere, Earl of Oxford, 23 knights, 44 squires and 63 archers.) Such retinues combined to make up the force which the chief tenant was bound to furnish the king, and the forces of all the chief tenants made up the army of the kingdom.

Sub-tenants holding less than a knight's manor were known as sergeants, i.e. mounted soldiers below the rank of knight. Sergeancy did not exist in England but on the Continent these men were required to provide a number of infantry in return for their land, or lead the local forces, or carry the lord's banner, their obligation depending on the size of their estate. They were equipped in the same manner as a knight but usually wore less armour and rode a lighter, unarmoured horse. These sergeants should not be confused with sergeants-at-arms, who were members of a royal bodyguard, originally formed by Philip Augustus of France but soon copied by other European monarchs. Sergeants-at-arms were used to carry orders, or to see that orders were carried out, and, together with the household knights of the king, formed an élite body of fighting men round the king's person. Until the emergence of standing armies they provided the nucleus for all armies raised by the king.

The kings of most countries also had the right to call out *en masse* all able-bodied men to serve as foot soldiers in emergencies. In England this was called the *Posse Comitatus*, the force of the county or shire, under the command of the sheriff. In the Holy Roman Empire the force was known as the *Heerban*; in France as the *Arrière-ban*. The men were usually required to arm themselves in accordance with their wealth, either as light infantry with bow or spear, or as medium infantry with a mail haubergeon or padded jacket, a steel helmet, and a spear and shield.

The length of service in the field owed by these forces varied slightly from country to country but on average was limited to forty days. Service could be extended by paying the troops, although many were reluctant to stay away from their lands for long periods and this made it exceedingly difficult to keep an army in the field for any length of time. The peasant levy was under no obligation to serve outside their own country and frequently up to two-thirds of the knights ignored the call to arms, preferring to pay fines or scutage tax, which allowed kings to hire a smaller number of professional soldiers in their place.

England, France, Sicily and southern Italy, the Scandinavian countries and the various duchies and counties of the Holy Roman Empire all followed this feudal system but because feudalism was based on a rural society it did not develop along the same lines in northern Italy and in Flanders, where the wealth and influence of the cities was often far greater than that of the lords. In fact many nobles abandoned their estates to take up trade in the rich cities, thus giving those cities control of the surrounding countryside. Florence, Venice and Genoa were such cities in Italy; Ypres, Ghent and Bruges in Flanders.

Light infantryman of the peasant levy armed only with a buckler and oncin, or pick; and a knight clad in mail hauberk, coif and hose, long surcoat and armed with the simple lance of the early fourteenth century. A great helm, or heaume, was worn over the coif for battle

Robert Rouse, Baron of Watre in Yorkshire, c. 1300. His mail is covered by a surcoat and reinforced by poleyns. The huge axe is the Eastern European bardische. It is unlikely to have been used by men-at-arms until c. 1450, though it was used by some infantry in the fourteenth century

These cities, and many other great cities in Europe, raised a third type of fighting man—the city militia. Unlike the feudal levy, the city militia was a regular force, for its duties included policing the city, garrisoning the city's castles, which protected the trade routes and ports, and guarding the borders of the state or republic. There may have been some form of conscription, or the militia may have been on a purely voluntary basis, but either way the men were better equipped and trained than the peasant levies and appear to have been rated the equal of professional mercenary infantry.

In Spain both the Spaniards and the Moors fought a war of lightning raids with plunder as their main objective and the Spanish knights therefore tended to wear lighter equipment than in the rest of Europe and to ride Arab horses. Cavalry below the rank of knight was armed only with a lance, javelins or darts, and a knife. The infantry consisted of spearmen, slingers and archers. This guerilla warfare drove the population from the land and in many ways Spain came to resemble northern Italy, with a number of more or less independent cities, but—unlike Italy—remaining under royal sovereignty. Because of

this, feudalism was never as strong in Spain as in England, France and Germany, although the number of knights available was considerably increased by the numerous Spanish and Portuguese military orders.

During the fourteenth and much of the fifteenth centuries Castile and Aragon were torn by civil wars and the cities raised militia forces for their own protection. These were known as the *Hermandades* in Castile, *Comunidades* in Aragon. This created a situation in which four different forces could be raised: those of the king, the barons, the military orders and the cities. The forces fought each other in various combinations.

The Mercenaries

In theory the feudal system enabled a king to call on large bodies of infantry and cavalry, but in practice neither force could be relied on. Apart from the failure to answer the call to arms and the difficulty of maintaining them in the field for more than forty days, those who did answer the summons often quarrelled amongst themselves, making it impossible to control the army as a unified body. The peasant levy was poorly equipped, untrained and, in an age when nationalism was still unknown, usually had no enthusiasm for war. As early as the end of the eleventh century military leaders recognised that no efficient army could be raised entirely by the feudal system and began to employ bands of mercenaries who were more efficient, better equipped and more willing to fight than the levies. These troops were mainly Brabançon spearmen and Gascon crossbowmen, equipped with mail hauberks, helmets and shields. By the middle of the twelfth century the infantry of most armies was stiffened by a substantial body of these mercenaries and by the end of the thirteenth century the payment of soldiers, whether they were mercenaries or levies, had become standard practice in order to maintain an army in the field for prolonged campaigns.

By the end of the thirteenth century the city states of northern Italy had exhausted themselves fighting each other for supremacy and relinquished their independence to local *signori* such as the Estes of Ferrara, Visconti of Milan and Medici of Florence. These *signori* soon found the city militias inadequate for the larger wars they now wished to wage to increase their territorial possessions, while the lack of an extensive feudal system meant there were comparatively few heavily armoured cavalry available. Therefore, in the first quarter of the fourteenth century the *signori* began to recruit bands of foreign mercenaries, mostly from Germany. These bands, known as *compagnie di ventura* (companies of fortune) consisted of between fifty and a hundred poorly armed men who reverted to their more usual occupation of brigandage at the end of their employment.

The first large, well equipped and disciplined force of mercenaries was the Great Company of 6,000 Germans and Swiss led by Werner von Urslingen. This company fought for various factions in Italy until 1351. An even larger but slightly later company was the Grand Company of Fra Moriale (he had been expelled from the Order of St John) which had 7,000 mounted men-at-arms and 2,000 crossbowmen. This emphasis on the heavy cavalry, supported by inferior numbers of crossbowmen and spearmen, is typical of most companies of fortune during the fourteenth and fifteenth centuries and reflects the essentially feudal character of Italian armies of this period.

In the second half of the century the Italians began forming their own companies, the most notable being the Company of St George led by Alberico, Count of Barbiano, and by the end of the century whole armies of such mercenaries were being raised. These mercenary armies endured in Italy until the end of the fifteenth century.

The captains of mercenary companies were highly skilled fighting men, often members of the *signori* families or their rivals for power. The size of their company depended on their reputation and the ability to raise money against that reputation. Employment was also governed by their reputation and the quality of the equipment of their men. The captains guaranteed their men's pay, even when the company was unemployed, and this arrangement was known as *condotta*, from which came the name *condottieri* for the captains.

In the same period that the *condotta* system was becoming established in Italy, the three Edwards of England were taking the first steps towards developing a purely mercenary army. Edward I (1272–1307) had attempted to increase the number of his cavalry by making all landowners with estates worth more than £20 a year render the service of a knight, but this move had been resisted. Edward III (1327–77) tried to raise a well equipped force of infantry by making communities pay their contingents of the shire levy, but this was also resisted by the people. Mercenaries were therefore employed on an increasing scale for the Welsh and Scottish wars of the late thirteenth and early fourteenth centuries. By the time of the Hundred Years War (1337–1453) English armies in France were composed almost entirely of paid men. However, the *Magna Carta* forbade the extensive use of foreign troops by a king of England and therefore these mercenaries were for the most part Englishmen—in effect a small but professional army of paid volunteers. The longbowmen were selected at village archery contests, the men competing for the honour of being chosen, a form of selective service unknown elsewhere in Europe.

In 1341 Edward III instituted a system of

A knight of the de Vere family, Earls of Oxford. (Quarterly, red and gold, the gold star indicating this is the heir of the earl.) He is armed in the style common during the first quarter of the fourteenth century

A knight of the early fourteenth century armed with sword, mace and dagger. The padded garment appearing below the hauberk is the aketon, a shirt-like garment of buckram stuffed with cotton, worn beneath the hauberk to support the mail and prevent broken links being driven into a wound.

written indentured contracts between the Crown and prominent captains, a method of raising a professional army which soon spread to most of northern and western Europe, becoming standard practice by the late fourteenth century and remaining in use until the emergence of standing armies. Under this system the captains contracted with the king to provide a certain number of men at a place of assembly by a set date. The contract set down precisely how long the men would have to serve, traditionally a minimum of forty days and a maximum of a year, their rates of pay, obligations and privileges. These companies usually contained men-at-arms, mounted and foot archers, and spearmen. The first instalment of their wages was normally paid by the captain

of the company, the king giving securities to repay the money at the mustering point or as soon after that date as possible.

In the fourteenth century neither France nor England had the financial resources to engage in prolonged warfare, yet the use of mercenaries for the campaigns of the Hundred Years War did create large armies, attracting men from all over Europe. Because these mercenaries had no means of earning a living except by war, they were extremely difficult to disband at the end of a campaign and the men who hired them were often forced to find them employment elsewhere in order to prevent their countries being overrun by brigands. After the French defeat at Poitiers (1356), resulting in the capture of the French king and the collapse of law and order, many of these bands, known as Free Companies, did resort to brigandage, having observed that the spoils of war were sufficient to make them rich without hiring themselves out to nobles and kings. These brigands usually established themselves in a stronghold and terrorized the surrounding countryside into paying tribute, capturing for ransom any wealthy travellers who passed through their area and sometimes uniting with other companies to sack a poorly defended town.

In an attempt to get these brigands out of France the Marquis of Montferrato hired many French, English and German companies in 1361 and attempted to seize the duchy of Milan. A large band known as the Guglers was taken to Switzerland by Enguerrand de Coucy, where it was almost annihilated by the men of Bern. Sir John Hawkwood took his White Company of 2,500 men-at-arms and 2,000 longbowmen into Italy, where he fought for Pisa, Milan and Florence until his death in 1394. The Great Company went to Avignon and forced the Pope to pay them large sums of money before Bertrand du Guesclin, later Constable of France, led them across the Pyrenees in 1364 to support Henry of Castile against Pedro the Cruel. The Black Prince hired other Free Companies and marched into Castile in 1367 to support Pedro and in the wars which followed the companies on both sides were practically exterminated.

These actions curbed the chaos in France but encouraged the spreading of Free Companies to other parts of Europe, where they often had a direct influence on subsequent events. Bands continued to plunder Brittany and Normandy and fight over the borders of Languedoc where, until the end of the Hundred Years War in 1453, 'English' companies could always be found to fight the troops of the king of France.

At the end of the Hundred Years War England was in chaos, the people rebelling against heavy taxes, the nobles settling their quarrels with private wars, and the rivalry between the Houses of York and Lancaster leading inexorably to the Wars of the Roses (1455–85). Many soldiers returning from France found employment in the private armies of the nobles. The king, lacking a standing army, was able to control disloyal nobles only by using the armies of those who remained loyal and this weakness in the royal authority led to corruption in the courts of law for, whenever the interests of a landowner were involved in a legal case, rival bodies of armed men would ride into the county town and intimidate witnesses, judge and jury.

Because justice was no longer obtainable for the small landowner, many of the yeoman farmers and lesser gentry turned to the great nobles for protection, entering into a contract known as Livery and Maintenance whereby they undertook to wear the noble's livery and badge and fight for him in times of need, and in return they would receive his protection whenever they needed it. These large private armies, and the contract troops raised by the Crown, formed the bulk of the fighting men for the Wars of the Roses, the royal or feudal levy being called out only at moments of great crisis.

The First National Armies

In 1291 the three forest cantons of Uri, Schwyz and Unterwalden in Switzerland formed a league against domination by the Houses of Habsburg and Savoy and in the fourteenth century the wars of emancipation from the Holy Roman Empire began which were to last until 1499. After the early victories Lucerne and Zürich joined the league to begin the formation of a confederation of peoples, speaking different tongues yet capable of welding themselves into one nation. In the first half of the fourteenth century this new nation forged a national army of peasant foot soldiers which was to prove capable of defeating in the open field time after time the chivalry of the Holy Roman Empire. After their decisive defeat of the Burgundians in the 1476–7 campaign the Swiss began hiring this infantry to other European countries and it soon became recognised as the élite infantry of Europe, superior to all other infantry and most cavalry until the sixteenth century.

No other national army emerged in Europe until 1419, when the Hussite Wars began between the people of Bohemia and the Holy Roman

Infantryman and knight of the first half of the fourteenth century. The infantryman is wearing a hauberk covered by a garment made up of multi-coloured leather flaps and some form of padded hose. The knight wears an early form of visored bascinet, his elbows are guarded by iron couters and his hands by gauntlets reinforced with iron plates and cuffs

Empire, again for religious and political freedom. The Bohemian chivalry was outnumbered by several hundreds to one, the peasants and burghers were poorly armed and undisciplined. The task of creating a national army from this unlikely material was given to Jan Ziska, who had acquired military experience fighting for the Poles against the Teutonic Order and more recently for the English at Agincourt (1415). Under his rigid discipline the entire adult male population of Bohemia was conscripted for military service, enabling large armies to be fielded by a comparatively small state. While half this army fought, the other half cultivated the land, rôles being reversed periodically. This army won more than fifty battles and minor actions in its first fourteen years, but its moral fibre was gradually weakened by the losses it suffered, casualties of necessity being replaced by mercenaries.

The French victories over the English in the 1430s, inspired by Joan of Arc, led to a truce which lasted from 1444 to 1449 and Charles VII used these quiet years to reorganise his forces. In 1439 under the *Ordonnance sur la Gendarmerie* he had made the first step towards a national army, led by royal officers and financed by a royal tax, and at the same time forbidden his nobles to raise troops without a royal licence. This provoked a rising amongst the nobles, which was crushed, leaving the king in a position of power and the way clear for France to become the first European nation to have a royal, standing army, as opposed to the 'people's armies' of Switzerland and Bohemia.

Charles' aim was to raise a police force to suppress the Free Companies and to provide a nucleus for an army with which to defeat any further English invasions. Amnesties were granted to the less villainous Free Companies and under the Constable de Richemont and the Comte de Dunois fifteen *Compagnie d'Ordonnance du Roi* were formed by 1445, each commanded by a noble chosen for his loyalty and military skill, the company being known by the name of its commander. These companies, later increased to twenty, formed the royal cavalry. They were lodged in strategic towns and cities and in peace time were paid by the provinces.

In 1448 another ordinance was passed which

A knight of c. 1330, showing how the plate armour was fixed on the arms. Beneath the short front of the surcoat may be seen the coat of plates and the hauberk, which was now cut away at the sides

Earl of Pembroke (died 1323) wearing the mixed mail and plate armour typical of the first half of the fourteenth century. The lower leg is now fully protected by a larger poleyn, greaves and sabatons (iron shoes): the shoulder reinforcement is a besague. The shield was suspended across the chest by the guige until the lance was broken, when the rein hand was transferred to other straps on the back of the shield

created an infantry militia—the *Franc-archiers*. Every group of fifty homes had to provide, equip and pay an archer or crossbowman, and by this ordinance Charles created a permanent, well armed and trained force of *c.* 8,000 infantry. During the same period the Royal Artillery was organised and trained by Gasper and Jean Bureau, who gave France the most technically advanced and effective artillery in Europe.

In the last campaigns of the Hundred Years War the infantry, cavalry and artillery of the Royal Army of France were victorious time after time, defeating the English in the field and recapturing castles and towns in rapid succession. At the close of the war France had a regular army of at least 12,000 men-at-arms and crossbowmen. For the invasion of Italy in 1494 this army was supplemented by Gascon crossbowmen and German and Swiss pikemen and halberdiers.

A different form of 'national' army was raised in Hungary in the second half of the fifteenth century. Hungary was ruled from 1309–82 by two Angevin kings, Robert and Louis, who strengthened the kingdom's military resources by introducing the feudal system, establishing military orders and raising a large bodyguard. These forces were the equal of the feudal cavalry of the Ottoman Turks until the early fifteenth century, by which date the Turks were using large numbers of infantry—the famous Janizaries, armed with the crossbow. (Suleiman the Magnificent, sultan from 1520–66, had about 12,000 Janizaries.) Since the Hungarians had no native infantry apart from the peasant levy, they began hiring mercenaries, mainly pikemen and arquebusiers. Matthias Corvinus, who dreamed of uniting central Europe under his rule, inherited this army when he became king in 1458 and from 1468 used it to make a series of conquests which gained him control of Bohemia, Moravia, Silesia and Austria. To help him conquer Austria, and hold on to what he had already gained, he organised a *standing* army of mercenaries, drawn mainly from Silesia and Moravia, known as the Black Army. This was financed by a tax which even the nobles, whose retinues formed the feudal army of the kingdom, were forced to pay.

In Spain Granada was retaken from the Moors by the *Reconquista* of 1481–91. The Spanish armies

A knight of 1325–30 wearing a decorated bascinet with a leather aventail to protect his neck, besagues, couters and studded gauntlets of textile. His arms are now protected by gutter-shaped plates, vambrace on the forearm, rerebrace on the upper arm, and the shoulders by overlapping plates called spaudlers. Note the aketon showing at the wrist. Under the shortened surcoat may be seen a coat of plates, a garment of iron plates held between two layers of cloth or leather by studs, worn over the hauberk as extra protection against the longbow.

English mounted and foot archers and crossbowman of about 1330–40. Men as well equipped as these would have been mercenaries hired for the Scottish wars of Edward III. The mounted archers used a longbow, not the short bow illustrated, and did not fire from horseback

of this period contained large numbers of feudal levies backed up by Swiss pikemen, German and Italian artillery specialists, English archers and billmen, French men-at-arms, and German arquebusiers. The militias of the cities were now united under the command of a royal officer to form the *Santa Hermandad*, the beginning of a national army, paid for by a tax not only on the burghers but also on the clergy and nobility.

The hiring of Swiss pikemen led the Spaniards to form their own companies of pikemen and these companies, stiffened by swordsmen, rose to such prominence that in the last decade of the century Spanish infantry were in great demand for the wars in Italy.

One other national army to emerge in the late fifteenth century was that organized by Maximilian I, king of Germany 1486–1519. Maximilian used as a basis for his army the mercenaries known as Landsknechts, who had formed bands of pikemen in imitation of the Swiss. When he came to the throne Maximilian issued commissions to his captains authorizing them to raise 'regiments' from the more respectable Landsknecht companies and during his reign he formed these mercenaries into an organized, well disciplined national army, encouraging his knights to serve in their ranks and nobles to lead them. When Maximilian was made Emperor of the Holy Roman Empire in 1493 he attempted to raise a standing Imperial army but the princes of the Empire refused to serve with the army or pay a tax to support it. The Landsknechts reverted to mercenaries and brigands after Maximilian's death in 1519.

Organisation

Medieval armies were normally divided into three divisions on the battlefield, the Vaward (or Vanguard), Main and Rearward Battles, with the light troops occasionally operating separately under their own commander. The Battles always marched in that order and normally deployed for battle with the Main Battle in the centre, the Vaward on the right and the Rearward on the left. (The Rearward Battle should not be confused with a rearguard, which was a force specially

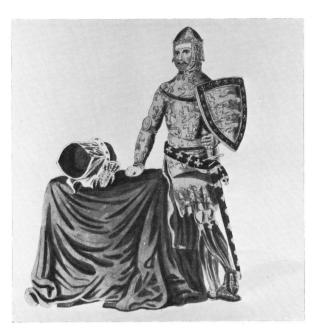

Earl of Cornwall (died 1329) from the effigy in Westminster Abbey. He is wearing a surcoat shortened in front, revealing the skirts of the various layers of body armour, while his limbs are protected by plate armour

selected to protect the rear of a retreating army.) Where there was insufficient room for such deployment the Battles might be placed with two in the front line and one in reserve, or in three successive lines. Smaller units operating within each Battle are described below.

THE CAVALRY

The smallest unit within the cavalry was the 'lance', not to be confused with a retinue, which also contained foot soldiers and was normally split up at the assembly point in order to group the troops into more convenient bodies of different arms. The English lance consisted theoretically of a knight, a man-at-arms and two mounted archers: Chaucer, writing *c.* 1360, mentions only a knight, a squire and one mounted archer. The French lance of 1450 contained a man-at-arms, a squire, and three mounted archers, or two mounted archers and a hobilar (light cavalryman). In Italy the earliest unit mentioned for the companies of fortune is a *barbuta* of a mounted sergeant and a man-at-arms. This was changed in the 1350s to a lance of a man-at-arms, a squire and a boy or page.

In Italy five lances made a *posta* and five *poste* a *bandiera* (flag), i.e. a unit of twenty-five cavalry.

According to a royal ordinance of 1351 the French cavalry was grouped in 'squadrons' (*routes*) of a fixed number, but the number is not mentioned. In England such squadrons varied from twenty-five to eighty in number, giving an average of about fifty, and were commanded by a knight flying a pennoncelle on his lance. In the Byzantine army the term for this commander was *Vintenaries*, suggesting fifty was the original number for a squadron. Byzantine military methods were studied in western Europe, both by reading extant Roman military writings and practical experience gained on crusade, and the rank of *Vintenary* is mentioned quite often in contemporary English documents.

Several such squadrons, perhaps making a total of from two to three hundred men, formed the equivalent of a modern cavalry regiment. At Bannockburn (1314) the 3,000 English cavalry were divided into ten 'battles', each of 300 men. These battles were then formed into the usual Vaward, Main and Rearward Battles, the cavalry in each case in three ranks, with the tenth battle acting as an advanced guard. The equivalent Byzantine formation was the bandon of 450 men: the *Compagnie d'Ordonnance du Roi* of the mid-fifteenth century contained 500 men; 100 lances of five. A 'regiment' was led by a knight bachelor, entitled to fly a pennon.

Two or three of these 'regiments' were usually united under the commander of a Battle, as at Bannockburn. Such a commander might be a king, prince or noble, all of whom could fly their personal banner and a standard for their troops to rally on. From the 1350s the command of a Battle was also given to knights below the rank of noble who had valuable military experience or could bring to the field of battle a large force of men. These commanders were known as knights banneret and were also permitted to fly a banner and standard.

The cavalry therefore consisted of nobles, knights, sergeants, squires, men-at-arms, hobilars and mounted archers, and some explanation is needed to clarify exactly what each of these terms means. The nobles and knights were of various ranks by which they may be positively identified: barons, counts, earls, dukes and princes in the nobility; and knights banneret, knights bachelor and simple knights. These men were the officers of the army, with the household knights and poorer knights fighting in the ranks. They and their horses were heavily armoured. The sergeants were all those below the rank of knight who had the equipment of a knight, or a lighter form of it. Their horses were smaller than those of the knights and were unarmoured.

Squires were apprentice knights, equipped in the same style as sergeants. The senior squire was known as the squire of the body and always accompanied his lord in battle, although two or three squires might go on campaign with each knight. Originally the squire's responsibilities were numerous: to assist his lord don his armour; hand him new weapons to replace broken or lost ones; supply a fresh horse if the lord was dismounted; take charge of any prisoners captured by the lord; rescue the lord if he was captured; carry him from the field if wounded; lend him assistance if he was attacked by several men at once; and act as subaltern to the retinue. However, there is evidence to suggest that after the middle of the fourteenth century most of these duties had become merely token ones, and squires were relied on to provide a force of medium cavalry with the sergeants.

The term man-at-arms actually applies to all mounted fighting men who wore armour, but although a knight might therefore be called a man-at-arms, a man-at-arms was not necessarily a knight, being possibly a sergeant or a squire. Thus the sergeants and squires, who normally fought in the ranks behind the first line of nobles and knights, formed the bulk—the rank and file—of the cavalry.

The light cavalry was represented by the hobilars, a term applied to unarmoured spearmen or archers mounted on small, light horses. They were used as despatch riders and scouts and normally played no part in the cavalry fighting. They were not cavalry in the true sense, being more akin to mounted infantry, using their horses only to get them to the scene of action, although they were sometimes used as light cavalry in pursuit of a defeated enemy.

Edward III created a mounted archer corps in 1334 in order to obtain greater mobility in the Scottish border wars. The tactical use of large

A knight of c. 1340 wearing black armour on his limbs. The cervelliere has developed into the more pointed bascinet, with mail aventail attached, and the heaume at his feet was now used only for tournaments. Note the rowel spurs, which replaced the prick spur, shown in preceding illustrations, about 1330. In Italy the bascinet was frequently worn without an aventail

Earl of Warwick (died 1370) wearing a shortened hauberk (haubergeon); jupon and plate armour, including cuisses on the thighs, which were common throughout Europe by this date. He was Marshal at Poitiers and is shown carrying the staff of office

numbers of archers supported by men-at-arms during the Hundred Years War made it essential that the two arms should be able to travel at the same speed and therefore during the fourteenth century an increasing number of English archers were mounted. By the second half of the century some French infantry were also mounted so that they might engage the highly mobile 'flying columns' of the English raiders.

There were three distinct types of horse in use at this time: the tall and heavy destrier, used only for tournaments; a poor breed of horse called a rounsey, which was ridden by all troops on campaign; and the courser, which stood about fifteen hands high and resembled a large show-jumper. The last was the war horse of the knight and was led by the squire (possibly the page boy, in fact) until battle became imminent, when the knight changed mounts.

THE INFANTRY

There were several distinct types of infantry: heavy infantry in the form of fully armoured, dismounted men-at-arms; the medium infantry of professional soldiers in half armour, such as crossbowmen, spearmen, and the city militias; and the light infantry of archers, unarmoured spear or javelin men, slingers, and the rabble of the levy armed with a variety of crude weapons, often nothing more than an agricultural tool mounted on a long haft.

The levy was mustered at various points in 'companies' but in battle these companies seem to have been merged to form a mass of light troops with little or no ability to manoeuvre in formation. Since they were normally kept to the rear they did not usually play a decisive part in a battle and were either massacred by the triumphant cavalry of the enemy or assisted in the pursuit and despatch of defeated infantry. If they could join in a cavalry mêlée they were quite deadly, hacking off men's legs with their polearms and axes, hamstringing the horses with their long knives or galling them with their spears. Before a battle commenced, bowmen, slingers and javelin men from the levy served in loose formation as skirmishers before the main battle line. The Swiss in particular placed great importance on skirmishers and frequently employed up to a quarter of their army in that rôle.

A knight of about 1380 dressed for the joust. The heaume is decorated with crest, wreath and scarf. In battle a visored bascinet would have been worn and the lance would have had a sharp point

The militia and mercenaries, who formed the hard core of the infantry, had a definite system of companies. The professional infantry of the French armies in the fourteenth century consisted of spearmen and crossbowmen, organized in companies of about thirty men, each company commanded by a constable who flew a pennoncelle on his lance. In English armies the infantry was also commanded by constables on occasions and at the end of the twelfth century a constabulary of Welsh infantry numbered 500 men, and this seems to have been a uniform size for infantry units of that time. (When the English army crossed the Somme prior to Agincourt the advanced guard consisted of 500 dismounted men-at-arms.

English longbowmen were organized in companies drawn from the parish areas under the command of a Master Bowman and the companies allocated to each of the three Battles were placed under the overall command of a knight or sergeant. During the reign of Edward III a corps of 120 archers called the Archers of the King's Guard was formed from the best bowmen in the kingdom, operating in conjunction with the sergeants-in-arms and the household knights. The French copied this idea in the second half of the century, raising a corps known as the Scottish Archers of the Guard.

The Swiss phalanx of pikemen was also formed of disciplined companies made up of men from each canton, a small division of territory similar to the English parish. The companies were grouped in three columns, the number of men in each varying according to the strength of the army; in the early days perhaps 500 men, later five or six thousand. Each canton elected its own captain and the commander of each column was elected by those captains.

The Hussite armies were organized with the wagon as the basic unit, each wagon and its driver being accompanied by ten pike and flail men to guard the gaps between the wagons, and ten archers, handgunners or crossbowmen positioned in the wagons themselves. The Landsknechts were organized in 'companies' of about 400 and these companies were grouped into three phalanxes like the Swiss. The Spanish infantry of the late fifteenth century was divided into 'colonelcies' of 1,000 men, divided into four companies of 250 men, one armed with sword and buckler, one with the pike, one with the arquebus and the fourth as light cavalry, or *ginetes*.

THE ARTILLERY

Although artillery did not become really effective until the fifteenth century it was used in battles and sieges as early as the 1320s and from the beginning took two distinct forms; siege guns and anti-personnel weapons. The siege guns of the fourteenth century and many of those of the fifteenth century were manufactured by welding iron bars together round a wooden core and securing them by shrinking on iron hoops, after which the wooden core was burnt out. One end of the tube thus formed was closed by an iron chamber holding a powder charge, held in place by a wedge between it and a barrier erected at the rear of the gun. These chambers were bottle-shaped, with an opening which lined up with the breech and a touch hole for firing the charge. Many guns had several chambers so that a fairly high rate of fire could be achieved. By 1430 such guns were being manufactured with calibres of 25 in., capable of firing stone balls weighing up to 400 pounds. Many of these larger guns were muzzle-loaders, the breech end blocked by a metal plug. The smaller guns were lashed to sledges for firing and transportation but the larger guns were fired lying on the ground, held in position by a framework of wooden beams, and were transported on carriages with iron-shod wheels. They were lifted on and off the carriages by crane.

Smaller muzzle-loading guns were cast in brass and in the 1320s are illustrated firing metal arrows. Another early form of anti-personnel cannon was the ribauldequin, a series of small

A knight of c. 1395 armed for battle. The chains on the breastplate were attached to sword and dagger hilt and first appeared in the 1360s. They were replaced soon after this date by the sword knot

cannon mounted on a wheeled carriage so that they could be discharged together by a sweep of a slowmatch. All these guns used a gunpowder which was mixed on the spot to prevent explosion or segregation of the ingredients during transportation. Loading a charge of this powder was a skilled task, for if rammed too tightly it would not ignite instantaneously, yet if packed too loosely it might fizzle out.

In the 1450s gunpowder was granulated to make it more stable but only the cast guns could withstand the greater force of this new explosive. Bronze guns were being produced throughout Europe by the 1440s and therefore during the second half of the century many long guns of small calibre were cast in bronze which fired a metal ball and relied on their high muzzle velocity for effect against fortifications. About 1470 these lighter, more mobile guns began to be cast with trunnions on each side which enabled the gun to be mounted on a wheeled carriage and acted as pivots to allow the gun to be elevated or depressed. The first really mobile field artillery accompanied Charles VIII on his invasion of Italy in 1494 and Fornova (1495) was probably the first battle where field artillery played a really decisive part, although it had been effective in the field since mid-century.

A derivative of the ribauldequin was the handgun, a small cannon fixed to a wooden stock, which came into general use about 1385. The early handguns were inaccurate and slow to load but in the early fifteenth century the gun was made much smaller, the stock shaped so that it could be held against the chest, and a trigger introduced for applying the slowmatch. This handgun was effective in volleys at close range but it was not until the introduction of the matchlock in mid-century that the arquebus, as it was now called, became a really effective weapon and provided an answer to the longbow and pike column. Companies of arquebusiers, mainly from Germany, fought in most of the European wars of the second half of the century.

MOVEMENT AND SUPPLY

The evidence available indicates that the logistics of war were fully understood in medieval times and were dealt with in much the same way as

A knight of about 1425. Arm and leg armour has changed little but the earlier body armours were replaced by a combination of mail and plate during the 1340–90 period. By the early 1420s the solid breast plate and fauld (skirt) were made of overlapping hoops (lames) to give greater flexibility. Italian faulds were often of mail only. This knight carries a war hammer, which became popular about 1450, and wears a helmet of the sallet style

staffs deal with logistic problems up to the utilization of railways for war. The men were obliged to arrive at the muster point by a certain date, equipped with their own weapons, armour and horses, and by and large medieval armies solved the provisions problem by living off the land, although English armies invading France usually took a small amount of food with them to allow the army to become established across the Channel. In Italy and Spain wars tended to be very destructive as far as agriculture was concerned and this caused greater problems of supply than in other countries. Most armies employed vast numbers of foragers, light infantry usually drawn from the peasant levy, to scour the countryside for food and horse fodder. The equipment of a medieval army was also comparatively simple and, although vast stocks of arrows or bolts were required, there was little of the paraphernalia of modern warfare, nor was there ever any concern about lines of communication except in the case of sieges.

The speed at which an army could travel was greatly restricted by the accompanying wagons and the lack of roads. Frequently the breakdown of a single wagon could delay the entire army. There were no accurate maps to assist in planning a campaign, and knowledge of the surrounding countryside, and of the enemy's movements, was supplied by scouts, local informers and deserters. It was not unusual for armies to fail to locate each other and this was one of the main reasons why commanders sometimes sent heralds to find the enemy and offer battle at a particular place on a set date. Freedom of movement was also restricted by castles and walled towns containing large garrisons, which either had to be besieged, causing a long delay, or by-passed at the risk of an attack in the rear. Such places were also used as a refuge by armies faced by a more numerous enemy, and once safely within such fortifications they could await the arrival of reinforcements, thus often bringing to nothing the concentration of forces for a decisive battle by a more able general.

Tactics

There are really only two ways of defeating an enemy once battle has been joined—shock tactics, in which an attempt is made to break the enemy by the violence and moral effect of a charge; or the use of missiles to destroy an enemy before he can get to close quarters, or drive him from the field if he assumes a defensive position. These two methods may be combined to produce different effects, but in the fourteenth century the emphasis was very much on shock tactics by the heavy cavalry, with small bodies of professional spearmen and crossbowmen in a supporting rôle only.

Large scale battles were quite rare in this period and many of the actions fought were little more than skirmishes between bodies of knights, where the main objective was to unhorse your opponent and put him to ransom, but in the larger battles the cavalry was divided into Battles, then again into squadrons, and supported by bodies of infantry. Successive charges were made by these Battles or their individual squadrons against different parts of the enemy line, each Battle or squadron rallying behind the professional infantry, where the crossbowmen were interspersed with the spearman and both took shelter behind the large shield of the latter. From this formation

Two knights of about 1430 wearing full plate armour, the one on the right wearing also a great bascinet; a visored bascinet with additional plates to protect the neck. The poleaxe held by the knight on the left was popular by mid-century

Henry VI of England c. 1430. The horse has a chanfron of plate on its head, in general use since the thirteenth century, and the king carries a shield designed to deflect lances from head and groin. After 1450 the shield was rarely used except for tournaments

the crossbowmen could fire on the enemy without fear of a cavalry attack, for the hedge of points presented by the spearmen effectively prevented any charge unless the tightness of the formation could be first loosened by missile fire.

These tactics were in general use in the first half of the fourteenth century, and continued to be used in many parts of Europe until quite late in the second half of the fifteenth century, but the introduction of the English longbow into Continental warfare in 1346 and the emergence of the Swiss pikeman in the early fifteenth century caused drastic changes in tactics.

THE ENGLISH LONGBOW
The longbow had been in use in South Wales and parts of England since at least the twelfth century but Edward I was the first to realise the full potential of the weapon during his conquest of North Wales. In 1282 he had 850 hired crossbowmen in his army but over the next decade this number dwindled to a mere seventy, while a large corps of longbowmen was trained to replace them. In 1292 at the Battle of Orewin Bridge his faith in this 'new' weapon was vindicated. The Welsh, mainly spearmen, had taken up a position

on the forward slope of a hill overlooking the bridge but just beyond bowshot, and any attempt to force a crossing by cavalry or infantry would have enabled them to descend at any time to engage as much of the English force as they chose, with the remainder unable to advance in support. However, at dawn the next day the English infantry crossed the river upstream by an unguarded ford and attacked the Welsh in the flank. The Welsh retired to make a stand on the hilltop. The cavalry was powerless against the hedge of spear points but the longbowmen were ordered forward and under a hail of arrows the Welsh ranks began to thin. Unable to break ranks to advance or retreat because of the cavalry poised for a charge, the Welsh were broken by the arrowstorm and the survivors ridden down by the cavalry. It was a perfect example of the combination of shock and missile tactics.

Edward took these tactics to Scotland and at Falkirk (1298) defeated 10,000 Scottish infantry and 200 knights with 12,500 infantry and 2,500 knights. The Scots took position on the forward slope of a hill, their front covered by a marsh, and formed four great hedgehogs of spearmen, with perhaps 2,000 archers in the intervals and the knights at the rear. It was impossible to cross the marsh and Edward's flank Battles therefore went round the ends, the Main Battle under Edward following to the right. The Scottish knights fled the field without striking a blow, enabling the English cavalry to ride down most of the archers, although they were repulsed by the spearmen with heavy losses. Edward then arrived on the scene and ordered forward the longbowmen. It was Orewin Bridge all over again and few of the spearmen survived the battle. The disaster at Bannockburn (1314), when 10,000 Scots defeated 23,000 English under Edward II, was the direct result of the cavalry attempting to fight the battle on their own.

These tactics were perfected during the early years of Edward III's reign at Dupplin (1332) and Halidon Hill (1333). At Dupplin 500 knights and 2,000 longbowmen faced a Scottish army of about 10,000. The English took position on a hill with the knights dismounted in the centre, except for a small mounted reserve, and the archers on the flanks, slightly forward so they could sweep the front with their fire. The Scottish spearmen attacked the men-at-arms in three columns but, weakened by the hail of arrows from the flanks, were halted by the thin line. Once halted the columns were almost useless and, becoming more and more crowded on the centre by the fire of the archers, were almost completely wiped out, the English reserve cutting down those who attempted to break away from the rear. At Halidon Hill Edward used the same tactics but remounted his cavalry to charge and break the Scots when their advance faltered in the face of the arrow-storm.

Realising it would be impossible to engage the far more numerous French chivalry in conventional cavalry battles, Edward employed the same tactics in the Hundred Years War, always ensuring his flanks and rear were protected against cavalry charges by natural obstacles. The French had taken no notice of events in Scotland, the naval disaster at Sluys (1340) where English longbowmen also won the day, or the small skirmishes at Morlaix (1342) and in 1345 when 500 men-at-arms and 2,000 archers helped the Gascons drive out invading French forces. Therefore, at Crecy (1346) the French, who had 35,000

Crossbowmen in the employ of France, 1430–70. Both are armed with the steel crossbow – the arbalest – which was not popular in the field until the second half of the century because longbowmen could fire twelve arrows in the time it took to reload an arbalest. Not much armour is worn because of the rise of arquebusiers. Note the infantry swords and cavalry shield

Sir John Cornwall portrayed holding a French banner captured at Agincourt. His squire holds Sir John's own banner. They are wearing the armour of the 1440s

men against 10,000 English—of whom only 1,141 were men-at-arms, attacked in fifteen successive waves of cavalry against the thin line of dismounted men-at-arms supported by longbowmen. The 5,500 longbowmen drove off the 5,000 surprised Genoese crossbowmen in the first minutes of the battle then concentrated on the horses of the French chivalry, shooting hundreds of the terrified animals, which trapped or injured many of their riders. Yet the longbowmen alone did not decide the battle, for some French did get through to engage the English men-at-arms in hand-to-hand fighting, though never in sufficient numbers to make any serious impression. At nightfall the French withdrew, having lost a third of their number.

The French refused to accept that the longbow had influenced the outcome of the battle and blamed their defeat on the fact that the English men-at-arms had fought dismounted. Therefore, when the two sides met again at Poitiers (1356) the French dismounted their cavalry, thus abandoning the only advantage the attacking men-at-

arms had—shock. The English did not have enough longbowmen this time to prevent the French closing and the first line was mainly defeated by the men-at-arms. However, the second French line retired from the field with the defeated first line, and when the third line began a long advance march Edward seized the initiative, just as at Halidon Hill, and remounting his men-at-arms charged the dismounted French. At the same time he sent a small cavalry force in a right hook to the French rear and after a fierce struggle the third line was also broken.

Edward III died in 1377 and under Bertrand du Guesclin the French began to recapture much of their lost territories. Du Guesclin realised that to defeat the English he need only control the key castles and towns and using an almost exclusively mercenary army he fought a war of harassment, ambushes and sieges, refusing to be drawn into open battle. Yet at Agincourt (1415) the French chivalry showed they had learnt nothing, attacking the English in a defensive position with three long lines of dismounted men-at-arms, virtually unsupported, and supported another disastrous defeat.

The successes of the French in the 1430s were not due to new tactics but mainly to the injection of fresh hope by Joan of Arc, who also taught them to attack the English before they could take up their customary impregnable position on a hillside. During the uneasy truce of 1444–9 the French organized their national army and at Formigny (1450) the longbow at last met its match. The English army of about 4,500 men was drawn up on a slope in its usual battle line but the French, who had slightly more men, did not make their customary assault. After two hours of skirmishing the French brought forward two culverins to enfilade the archers' position and began to mow them down from beyond bowshot. Some of the archers broke ranks and charged the guns, overrunning them, but the French men-at-arms were now able to charge home and at close quarters made short work of the archers.

No other country adopted the longbow, primarily because a longbowman needed constant practice to reach and maintain efficiency. This meant he had to have his own bow and arrows, not weapons drawn from an arsenal in times of crisis, and few European countries dared to permanently arm their peasants for fear of rebellion. However, English archers fought in many parts of Europe with the Free Companies. The first battle in which both sides possessed longbowmen was Shrewsbury (1403) where the rebel forces of the Percys met Henry IV. The Percys' army of 10,000 men was drawn up on a hill with the archers in front and the battle began with the archers of Henry's 30,000 strong army advancing up the hill. The Percy's archers were more numerous and after a shattering exchange of fire the king's archers broke and ran down the hill, followed by the Percys' men-at-arms. The royal army was forced back but, because it was much larger, it overlapped the flanks of the rebels and was able to curl round one flank and attack them in the rear. Hotspur Percy was killed and the rebels broke and fled. It is important to note that the battle was decided by the men-at-arms, not the archers, and that when both sides had the longbow the main victims of the arrows were the archers themselves. During the Wars of the Roses the same rule applied and both sides were usually compelled to close for a mêlée as soon as possible.

THE SWISS PIKE

At the same time that the longbow was rising to prominence another infantry weapon was emerging which was to help bring about the downfall of the heavy cavalryman—the polearm. For two and a half centuries companies of spear-men had been used to support the cavalry. In the thirteenth century companies of Brabanters armed with a longer, twelve-foot spear were hiring them-selves out to France, England and Italy. At Courtrai (1302) 20,000 men of the city militias of Flanders defeated a French army of 50,000 with the help of these long spears, bills and other polearms. At Bannockburn (1314) the English were defeated by the Scots—the majority of whom were armed with the twelve-foot spear. At Mortgarten (1315) the forest cantons of Uri, Schwyz and Unterwalden fought their first battle against their oppressors and used their halberds with devastating effect against the feudal cavalry of Duke Leopold I of Austria, utterly routing the Austrian chivalry.

In all three of these battles the cavalry was

A knight in the full plate armour of the 1440s. The fauld was altered about 1430, the lower part being separated into two plates, the tassets. About the same date the shoulder pieces, now called pauldrons, became larger and had their inner edges turned up to protect the neck. These turn ups were called haute pieces. Note the extra plates on the left arm to replace the shield

A knight of about 1445 in full plate armour and holding the poleaxe, which was now in general use by knights fighting on foot

Richard, Duke of York, who died at the Battle of Wakefield (1460). The globular breast plate returned to favour about this date, as did the huge two-handed sword illustrated, particularly with the Landsknechts and Swiss

seriously hampered by the terrain: marshes at Courtrai and Bannockburn, ambushed in a narrow defile at Mortgarten. On open ground, at Mons-et-Pevele (1304) and Cassel (1328), the Flemish infantry were cut to pieces by the French chivalry, just as the English annihilated the Scottish spearmen at Falkirk. This was primarily because the spearmen of this date lacked speed and manoeuvrability: although they were strong on the defensive they could not change front or formation easily and because of these limitations they could rarely win a battle on their own.

After Mortgarten the forest cantons received support from the Swiss of the lower alpine lands, who brought to the 'national' army a 'new' weapon—the pike. At this time the pike differed from the twelve-foot spear only in having a lighter head, and it was used in the same manner as the spear. However, the Swiss were not content merely to assume a defensive attitude and as a result of intense training and tight discipline developed the ability to manoeuvre so swiftly that they could take the offensive even against cavalry. They were helped in this by the lightness of their equipment, poverty preventing them from being slowed down by body-armour.

The new army was first tested at Laupen (1339) where it met the Burgundian army in the open field. The Swiss formed three columns, the pikes on the right and in the centre, the halberds of the forest cantons on the left. The Burgundian infantry opposing the pike columns was soon trampled down and driven from the field but the Burgundian chivalry attacked the forest cantons in successive waves and inflicted heavy losses, the halberds being too short to prevent the cavalry closing. The forest cantons fought back grimly and held the Burgundian cavalry until the two pike columns could turn and advance to their support. Finding themselves unable to press home a charge against the advancing pike columns, the Burgundian cavalry then rode from the field.

At Sempach (1385) Duke Leopold, probably remembering the ineffectiveness of cavalry against pikes at Laupen, dismounted his Vaward Battle to engage the leading column of the Swiss army. He kept his other two Battles mounted, believing one Battle sufficient to defeat the Swiss column, for the main body of the Swiss was not yet within supporting distance. The Swiss were almost defeated but Leopold had not allowed for the rapidity of a Swiss advance and the main body now arrived and threw back his Vaward

**Walter von Hohenklinger, German
knight, early fourteenth century**

GERALD EMBLETON

A

**Guidoriccio da Fogliana, Condottiere, early
fourteenth century**

Joan of Arc, 1429–30

GERALD EMBLETON

C

1 Spearman, 1300–1400
2 Peasant Levy, 1300–1400
3 Crossbowman, 1300–1400

D

1 **Hand-gunner, 1460–1500**
2 **English billman, 1400–1450**
3 **English longbowman, 1350–1450**

GERALD EMBLETON

E

F

GERALD EMBLETON

1 Swiss pikeman, 1339–1500
2 Spanish infantryman, 1481–1500
3 English Archer of the Guard, 1485–1500

GERALD EMBLETON

G

Identification and description of these flags is on page 40

Battle. Leopold hurriedly dismounted his Main Battle and led them forward but they were disordered and before they could arrive the Vaward Battle broke, the third line of Austrians rode from the field, and Leopold and his Battle were surrounded and slaughtered.

At Arbedo (1422) the Italians also used dismounted men-at-arms, 6,000 in a single column against a Swiss phalanx of about 4,000, of whom two-thirds were armed with halberds, only one-third with pikes and crossbows. The Swiss were on the verge of defeat when 600 of their foragers appeared in the rear of the Italians. Mistaking them for reinforcements, the Italians drew off and the Swiss took the opportunity to retire from the field. Mainly because of this experience the Swiss now adopted the pike as their main weapon, but with a fifteen-foot haft. Halberdiers were retained to guard the cantonal banners and if a column was halted these troops issued from the sides and rear of the column to attack the enemy's flanks and break the deadlock. Their reputation as the finest infantry in Europe was established at St Jacob-en-Birs (1444) where less than 1,000 Swiss pikemen attacked a French army outnumbering them by fifteen to one. The Swiss were all killed, but fought to the last man and took 2,000 of their enemies with them. From that date the Swiss remained superior to all other infantry and fully capable of withstanding the finest cavalry, and even defeating it.

The usual order of battle employed by the Swiss was an advance in echelon of three columns, the leading column making for a fixed point in the enemy line while the central column marched parallel and slightly to the left or right rear. The third column was still further back and frequently halted when the first column struck to observe the result before becoming committed. There were a number of variations of this battle order. Sometimes the centre column would lead and both flanks would be refused, or the two flanks advanced and the centre refused. The strength of the columns increased as more cantons supported the league but sometimes the emphasis would be on the right and centre with only a small column on the left, or on occasions there would be an enormous right hand column and a small left and centre. The columns could advance very rapidly for over a mile with their pikes levelled and this speed often enabled them to force an enemy to fight where and when they chose.

The Swiss columns did not suffer the fate of the Flemish and Scottish spearmen because of their manoeuvrability and because they were always preceded and supported by light troops who formed from ten to twenty-five per cent of the army. At first these troops were armed with the crossbow but as early as the battle of Näfels (1388) handguns were being used and these gradually replaced the crossbow during the fifteenth century.

After defeating the Burgundians in the 1476–7 campaign the Swiss began hiring themselves out as mercenaries and served in most of the European

A knight and sergeant-at-arms of about 1470. The knight would have worn a sallet. The sergeant is wearing a simple steel cap, breast plate and large poleyns only. The large hilt of his sword suggests he is armed with a two-handed sword as well as the plain lance of the medium cavalry. (The head should be more slender)

wars of the late fifteenth century, now using an eighteen-foot pike. Because they struck with a shock almost equal to that of heavy cavalry only another column of pikes could stand up to them but although many countries formed corps of pikemen none could withstand the Swiss during the fifteenth century. The only successful opponents of the pike in this century were the Spanish, who mixed a strong force of sword and buckler men with their pikemen. A Spanish column consisted of pikes in the front ranks with arquebusiers at each flank, and sword and buckler men behind the pikemen ready to cut down the enemy pikemen once they had been halted. The Spanish infantry rose to a position of prominence towards the end of the century and were in great demand for the wars in Italy, but they did not encounter any Swiss pikemen until the battle of Barletta (1502) where the sword and buckler men got beneath the pikes and slaughtered the lightly armoured Swiss at close quarters.

THE HUSSITE WARS

Another system of tactics developed in the fifteenth century which proved capable of defeating feudal cavalry and levies was that devised by Jan Ziska,

Henry VII of England in a damascened armour which follows civilian fashions. The horse armour is in the Tower of London armouries. The infantryman is wearing a brigandine reinforced by metal plates, held in place by the studs, and carries a short sword and typical fifteenth century bill. He wears a sallet, which was very popular in England

26

An English man-at-arms of 1483 in full armour. Such an equipment weighed about seventy pounds but the weight was distributed over the whole body and the main disadvantage of the armour was not the weight but the stuffiness inside it. Because such equipment was very expensive, in the second half of the century simple knights and the rank and file of armies wore either partial plate with mail, as in the fourteenth century, or the fabric body armours of the same period

commander of the Puritan Hussite army of Bohemia during the wars with the Catholic Holy Roman Empire. The Czech nobility faced the same problem as that of England in 1337—the cavalry of their enemies outnumbered them by several hundreds to one. Therefore, again like the English, and indeed the Swiss, the people had to be organized into an infantry force capable of standing up to feudal cavalry, even though virtually unsupported by cavalry. Ziska had seen the *goliaigorod* (moving fortress) used by the Russians when attacked on the march; the drawing into a circle of the wagons accompanying the army to form a barrier against cavalry. Ziska copied this idea, at first using any carts and wagons he could obtain, but later having specially reinforced wagons constructed which carried small cannon and were fitted with heavy chains to link them together. Within these moving fortresses his

peasants and burghers were safe from the numerous cavalry of the Holy Roman Empire and with a combination of polearms and missile weapons were quite capable of dealing with the feudal levies or dismounted men-at-arms.

In the early battles Ziska relied entirely on the defensive strength of his *wagenberg* but soon, by discipline and extensive training, he was able to turn the *wagenberg* into an offensive weapon, just as the Swiss had advanced the use of their pike. A special corps of wagoners was formed which could manoeuvre the wagons into a circle, square or triangle at a single word of command, disengage the teams and chain the wagons together, all under the noses of an army rendered slow in manoeuvre by the disunities of the feudal system. From the very beginning Ziska also made use of handguns; almost one-third of the missile men in the wagons had firearms; and the *wagenberg* was supported by a strong train of artillery which included cannon capable of throwing projectiles weighing up to 100 pounds.

The basic order for a Hussite army on the march was five parallel columns; the cavalry and artillery in the centre, flanked on each side by two divisions of wagons with their complements of infantry. The two inner wagon columns were shorter than the outer ones and at a word of command could be moved rapidly into position at the head and rear of the army to form a rectangular defensive formation.

The Holy Roman Empire responded to its first defeats by raising an even larger army instead of seeking new ways of dealing with this new weapon, and in January 1422 a great army under the Emperor Sigismund was decisively defeated at Nemecky Brod. Sigismund was defeated again at Nebovid, Kutna and Hora that year but the following year there was civil dissension in Bohemia, the people dividing into the Taborite extremists under Ziska and the moderate party, including the nobility, known as the Utraquists. Ziska defeated the Utraquists at Hŏric and Strachov that year, and at Skalic and Malesov in 1424, dying later that year of the plague.

A priest called Prokop took command of the Taborite army and at Aussig (1426) and Tachau (1427) defeated the forces of the Holy Roman

Empire. The reputation of the Taborites was now such that the German levies often could not be made to attack the *wagenberg* and, gaining experience and courage from their invincibility, the Taborites took to advancing from the *wagenberg* to defeat armies numerically their superior. In 1429 Prokop invaded Saxony and bands of only a few thousand men laid waste to Bavaria, Meissen, Thuringia and Silesia. At Domazlice (1431) they defeated the papal forces of Cesarini and in 1433 a force under Jan Czapko raided the Teutonic Knights' Ordensland in retaliation for supporting Sigismund, sacking Dirschau and Oliva.

The only real threat to the *wagenberg* was cannon fire at the wagons themselves, but the Taborite artillery was always strong enough to silence the enemy's guns and it was not the Holy Roman Empire which finally defeated the *wagenberg* but the Czechs themselves. At Lipan (1434) the Taborites led by Prokop again met the Utraquists. The moderates attacked the *wagenberg* and were

Sir John Cheney, standard bearer to Henry VII at the Battle of Bosworth (1485), the last battle of the Wars of the Roses. He carries Henry's green and white banner charged with a red dragon

repulsed but the Taborites, forgetting they were no longer fighting the levies of the Emperor, rushed out to pursue the fleeing Utraquists, who then turned and began to fight back fiercely. The Utraquist cavalry reserve easily defeated the small Taborite force of cavalry and swiftly cut off the Taborites from their *wagenberg*. The extremists were then cut to pieces on the open field by the cavalry, only a few thousand who had remained within the *wagenberg* surviving. They never recovered from this battle and their city of Tabor fell to the Utraquists in 1452.

Lipan illustrates the basic weakness of the *wagenberg*: unlike the longbow and pike it was a purely defensive weapon, successful only against the out-dated, unthinking tactics of a feudal host. Against steady troops commanded by an intelligent and experienced general it could be rendered ineffective.

In the sixteenth century Henry VIII of England mounted some of his arquebusiers in armoured wagons but otherwise the Taborite tactics were not employed elsewhere in Europe, although the *wagenberg* was known. For example, when in 1429 Sir John Fastolf, *en route* to the besiegers' lines at Orleans with a train of provisions, was attacked by 8,000 men-at-arms, he drew the wagons into a circle and easily repulsed the French attacks with his small force of 2,000 archers and spearmen.

THE CONDOTTIERI

Because Italian armies of the fifteenth century were composed of *condottieri*, feudal tactics persisted in Italy until the end of the century. Most of the wars between the city states and republics were economic in motive and the captains of the mercenaries therefore tended to regard war as a business and their men as their capital. Since today's enemy might be tomorrow's comrade in arms, there was little point in fierce, bloody battles where friends might be killed and the captain's capital severely diminished, thus endangering the future of the company. Therefore, the *condottieri*, who were mostly heavily armoured cavalry, usually fought only in the summer, away from the mountains and marshes which were so inconvenient for cavalry, and avoided pitched battles as much as possible. A great deal of time

Early fourteenth century man-at-arms wearing helm of previous century. The horse armour is of leather and scale armour for lightness, with a plate chanfron. Note the metal plates on the saddle and the greaves

was spent burning crops and destroying vineyards and orchards, for the ability to wage war depended on money, which meant a thriving commerce and agriculture: if you could destroy an enemy's crops and restrict trade by besieging his cities and ports, you crippled his ability to maintain a mercenary army in the field. Such methods were effective and much safer than pitched battles.

When a pitched battle was unavoidable it often resembled a leisurely game of chess, perhaps culminating in a cavalry mêlée and a brief exchange of battering blows on each other's armour, after which the out-manoeuvred commander conceded defeat and withdrew from the field. The emphasis was on the traditional dismounting of an opponent for ransom rather than the evolution of new tactics. At the battle of Zagonara (1423) only three men were killed: at Molinella (1427), which lasted all day, some horses were killed and men taken prisoner, but no man died.

This type of warfare received a rude shock in 1439 when many Venetians were killed by arquebusiers in the employ of Bologna. So great was the outrage at this 'atrocity' that when the Venetians won the day they executed all those who had carried firearms. Towards the end of the century Italy became the battle field for French, Spanish and German armies equipped with the pike, longbow, crossbow, arquebus, disciplined squadrons of men-at-arms and highly mobile artillery—all designed to kill the enemy. By 1500 the *condottieri* were fast disappearing from the battlefield before such ruthless warfare and with them went the last vestiges of the old feudal tactics and the belief that the heavily armoured cavalryman ruled the battlefield.

The Plates

A Walter von Hohenklinger, German knight, early fourteenth century

von Hohenklinger is dressed for the tourney but at this date most feudal cavalry took the field dressed in a similar fashion. The flat-topped heaume was replaced by a more conical version towards the end of the 13th century but it was not uncommon for many pieces of a knight's

Man-at-arms wearing full plate equipment of the second half of the fifteenth century, riding a horse protected by a leather and plate bard. The 'breast plate' (peytral) and neck piece (crinet) were introduced during the fourteenth century

equipment to remain in use after the introduction of new fashions because of expense. Under the heaume was a mail coif, and under that an arming cap to prevent chafing and protect the head against heavy blows. The large crest is typical of those worn by German knights. Crests were popular in Germany, England and the Low Countries, but rare in France, Italy, Spain and Portugal. The body is protected only by a mail hauberk and hose, although in other countries plate reinforcements to the leg were common by this date. The wooden 'heater' shield was slightly curved, about 95 cm. long by 15 mm. thick. The sword is typical of the Middle Ages up to *c.* 1320; 33–36 in. long, three to four pounds in weight, with a double-edged blade and the wheel pommel which remained popular throughout the 1300–1500 period. Walter von Hohenklinger was killed at the battle of Sempach in 1385.

B Guidoriccio da Fogliana, Condottiere, first half fourteenth century

In the early fourteenth century the *condottieri* were professional soldiers, sometimes of the nobility, but more often adventurers seeking a fortune, who hired themselves and their brigands to the highest bidder. The *condottieri* of the late fourteenth and the fifteenth centuries were frequently princes who, between their own wars, hired their armies to other states and republics in order to keep the troops in full employment. The mail worn by Fogliana, reinforced by plate armour on the legs, is typical of the first half of the fourteenth century; plate armour was rarely worn on the arms in fourteenth-century Italy. Textile horse-trappers were introduced in the twelfth century to protect the horse against the weapons of the infantry and by the thirteenth century were often reinforced with plates of metal or horn, or padded and quilted, or made of leather. The trapper was in two halves, meeting at the saddle.

C Joan of Arc, 1429–30

By 1410–20 the knight was wearing an armour made entirely of plate, although mail continued to be used in the fifteenth century by the lesser knights and rank and file of armies. Italian armours frequently had mail sabatons and a mail skirt instead of the plate fauld. Plate armour began to replace the textile horse-trapper at the end of the fourteenth century and by *c.* 1430 the horse bard of all-plate had been introduced, although hardened leather (*cuir bouilli*), shaped to look like metal plates, was often used because of its cheapness and light weight.

(1) Fifteenth century helmet and brigandine. (2) Late fifteenth century greave and sabaton. (3) Gauntlet of the second half of the fourteenth century. (4) Fifteenth century gauntlet. (5) Gorget to protect the neck, often worn with the early fourteenth century kettle hat and, by c. 1410, with the bascinet. (6) All metal mace of the early fifteenth century. (7) Prick spur, 1300–30

31

(1 & 2) Concave 13 in. diameter buckler of wood covered with leather and decorated with nails. The boss projects four inches.
(3 & 4) Bardische head and butt ferrule. (5 & 6, 7 & 8) Late fifteenth century poleaxes and butt ferrules. Hafts were from
four to five feet long, giving an overall length of five to six feet

D1 Spearman, 1300–1400

The professional spearman wore a hauberk and carried a targe, about two feet long, or the longer pavise. The light yet strong kettle hat was popular with infantry throughout the 1300–1500 period and was also worn by knights, sometimes on top of the cervelliere or globular bascinet. The short spear was a major infantry weapon of the fourteenth century, used like a bayonetted rifle for the charge or to form a hedge of points when on the defensive. It had a five foot haft and twelve inch broad bladed head. The spear used by the Scots and Brabanters in the first quarter of the century was between ten and twelve feet long, with a more slender head. Secondary weapon was usually a long dagger.

D2 Peasant Levy, 1300–1400

Feudal armies, such as the French ones of the Hundred Years War, frequently had up to fifty per cent of their strength in peasant levies, who were used for camp duties, foraging and skirmishing. In defeat they were at the mercy of the pursuing cavalry—as were the mercenaries—but if they got amongst the cavalry during a mêlée they could be so deadly that trappers had to be used to protect the horses, and knights had to wear more and more complex leg armour to protect themselves against the long knives, axes and polearms of the peasantry. Other weapons used by the levies were clubs, bows, spears, and agricultural tools.

D3 Crossbowman, 1300–1400

The best companies of crossbowmen came from Genoa, Gascony and the Low Countries. They usually wore a haubergeon, simple steel helmet and plate reinforcements on elbows and knees. The composite bow was used in the field throughout the 1300–1500 period and had an accurate range of sixty yards. Four to six longbow shafts could be discharged in the time it took to load a crossbow, which also lacked the penetrative power of the longbow. Secondary weapon was a long knife or a small axe. The arbalesters of the second half of the fifteenth century wore little or no armour.

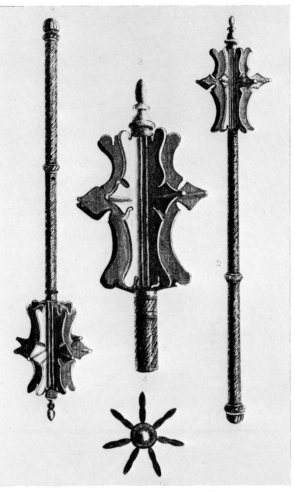

All iron mace of the second half of the fifteenth century. Weight three pounds nine ounces; length 25 inches; head seven inches. The handle is hollow

E1 Hand-gunner, 1460–1500

The hand-gunner illustrated is armed with an all-iron gun, apparently fired in the same manner as a modern bazooka. The illustration is based on a figure in a siege scene in a medieval manuscript, and the weapon may be designed purely for siege work. Certainly by the mid-fifteenth century genuine handguns, or arquebuses, were being produced with a wooden stock which was held against the shoulder, a barrel with a calibre of about one inch, and a spring-loaded mechanism for the slowmatch. They were effective in volleys at close range. Maximum range was four hundred yards, effective range about two hundred yards, accurate range considerably less. Rate of fire was between eight and ten shots an hour.

Venetian poleaxe of about 1530, very similar to the types used in the second half of the fifteenth century

a hook at the back and sometimes a spike at the top, was popular throughout the fifteenth century, especially in England, France and Italy. Secondary weapon was a sword or small axe. The spearman's shield was abandoned because both hands were needed for polearms. Billmen wore a variety of helmets; a bascinet and aventail as illustrated — probably picked up on the battlefield or handed on by a knight, a kettle hat, or in the second half of the century a sallet. Their bodies and limbs were protected by the haubergeon, sometimes with plate reinforcements on arms and legs. The illustrated figure bears the hound (talbot) of the Talbot family, Earls of Shrewsbury, on his tunic, which is in the livery colours of that family. The use of such badges was never so widespread or important in Europe as in England.

E3 English longbowman, 1350–1450
The longbowman sometimes wore a haubergeon, or a quilted jacket, but frequently was protected by only a leather jerkin or wore no body armour at all. The cervelliere and kettle hat were popular forms of helmet, though some archers wore only a felt hat. Secondary weapon was usually a dagger or the maul, though in the fifteenth century some carried swords. The wooden buckler was held at arm's length for parrying blows in a mêlée. The longbow was about six feet long and required a pull of eighty pounds. Flight arrows were about 37 in. long and were used for high trajectory, long range firing: the more sturdy sheaf arrows were about 27 inches long and were used at close range for piercing mail and occasionally plate—if a square hit could be obtained. Longbowmen usually protected their front against cavalry by digging pitfalls (Crecy) or erecting stakes (Agincourt). The archer illustrated wears the badge and livery of the de la Pole family, Earls of Suffolk.

F1 Infantryman, 1460–1500
Most infantry of the second half of the fifteenth century were armed with some form of polearm, in this case a partizan, a development of the spear which originated in Italy in the early part of the century. The partizan, with its thirty-inch, double-edged blade for cut-and-thrust, and lugs for breaking or entangling sword blades, soon

E2 English billman, 1400–1450
The agricultural bill was used as an infantry polearm in the fourteenth century but from the beginning of the fifteenth century it is noticeable that bodies of infantry formerly referred to as spearmen were now termed billmen. The bill, different from the agricultural tool only in having

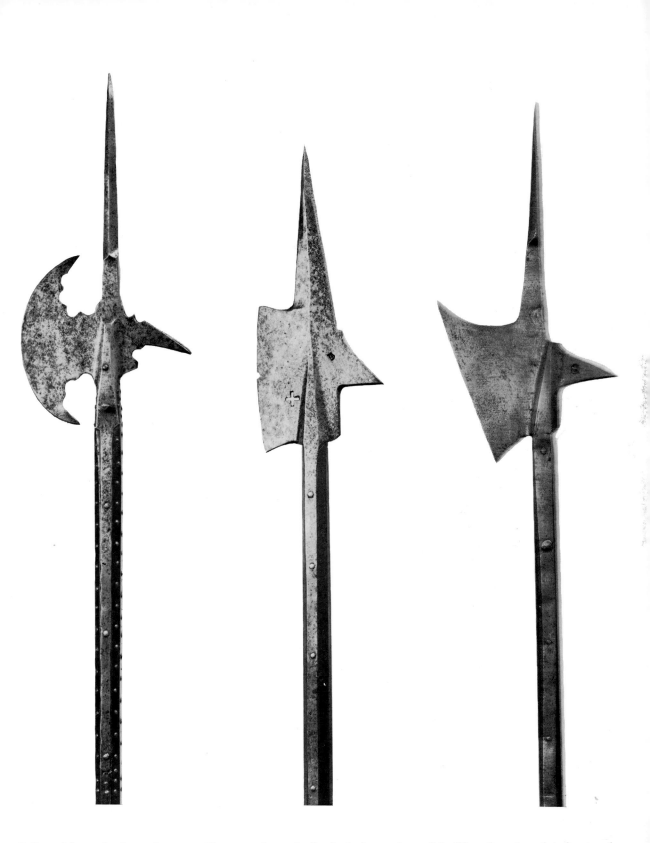

Left to right: early sixteenth century German poleaxe similar in design to those of the fifteenth century; late fourteenth, early fifteenth century Swiss halberd of the type used at Sempach; German halberd of about 1500, typical of the kind carried by German and Swiss infantry at the end of the fifteenth century

Early fifteenth century bombard of wrought iron with 15-in. calibre, firing a stone shot weighing about 160 pounds. The carriage is modern

spread throughout Europe. The illustration shows typical armour for infantry of the time; a brigandine, similar to the jack but with smaller plates for greater flexibility, and a long 'tailed' German sallet with pivoted visor. The Italian sallet had a short 'tail', as did the German one after about 1480.

F2   Gunner, 1450–1500

Gunners usually carried only a dagger and wore the fabric body armours of the infantry and poor knights; a canvas, leather or textile jack or brigandine, reinforced by metal plates. The cannon illustrated is a muzzle-loading, wrought-iron bombard of the 1330–1470 period, firing a stone ball. By the mid-fifteenth century such cannon were used mainly for siege warfare, and the wooden stand is typical of this period.

F3 French man-at-arms, 1450–1500

The poleaxe was the favourite weapon of dismounted men-at-arms from *c.* 1450 but the two-handed axe illustrated here was also popular throughout Europe until the end of the century.

Despite its size the head of such an axe weighed only about three pounds. The man wears the simple globular bascinet which remained popular in France and Italy, a full equipment of plate, and on his tunic is the winged hart badge of the House of Bourbon, although Bourbon livery colours were white and green.

A wrought iron, breech loading peterara of the time of Edward IV (1461–83) complete with powder chamber, which has a lifting handle and vent hole. Note wedge for jamming the bottle shaped chamber into the breech

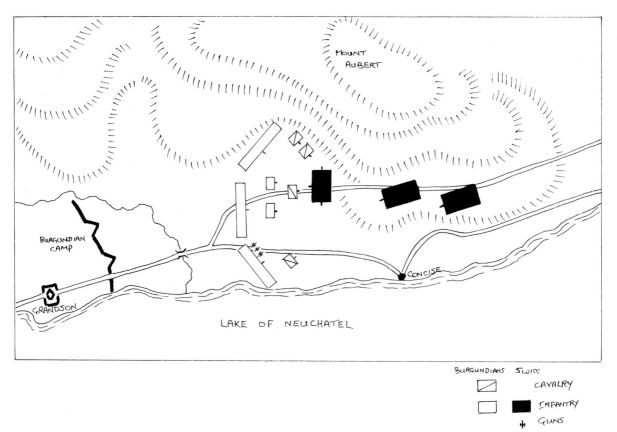

MOUNT AUBERT

BURGUNDIAN CAMP

LAKE OF NEUCHATEL

CONCISE

GRANDSON

	BURGUNDIANS	SWISS	
	▨		CAVALRY
	▢	■	INFANTRY
		⸦⸧	GUNS

GRANDSON 1476 One of the three major battles of the Burgundian campaign of 1476–77 against the Swiss. Here Charles the Bold attempted the classic double envelopment of Hannibal at Cannae, but the infantry on his flanks, seeing the rapid advance of two more Swiss columns and mistaking the withdrawal of the centre for a retreat, broke and fled in panic. Prime cause of this panic was a lack of cohesion between the various units of the Burgundian army; a common failing in feudal armies

G1 Swiss pikeman, 1339–1500

Because of poverty the Swiss pikeman was originally protected only by a simple helmet and a leather jerkin, and so few men had breastplates that only the front rank of a phalanx had any armour. Officers were usually fully armoured and mounted, although they dismounted to fight. In the second half of the fifteenth century more men had breastplates and fully armoured men were placed in the front rank. Sallets were worn by this date, and tunics and hose were striped or parti-coloured but tight fitting; the slashed, loose clothing usually associated with the Swiss not becoming common until the sixteenth century. When on the defensive the first four ranks of a phalanx levelled their pikes while those to the rear kept their pikes upright, ready to replace a fallen comrade. The first rank knelt with the pike held low, the butt on the ground behind them: the second rank stooped with the butt under their right foot: the third rank held the

pike at waist level: and the fourth rank held it at head level. For the advance the pikes were held horizontally at chest level, right arm back and left arm forward, with the head of the pike pointing slightly downwards. The Landsknechts copied this drill but pointed their pike heads slightly upwards.

G2 Spanish infantryman, 1481–1500

Spanish sword and buckler men wore a tall cabacete with a turned-down brim, drawn up front and rear, with a bevor to protect the lower half of the face, and a full equipment of plate armour. They were armed with a short, straight, double-edged thrusting sword and a dagger. The wooden buckler had a diameter of ten to twelve inches and was reinforced with nails and metal.

G3 English Archer of the Guard, 1485–1500

The Archers of the Guard were formed by Edward III (1327–77) and apparently perpetuated by Henry VII, who in 1485 formed the Yeomen of the Guard, a bodyguard of fifty archers under a captain, increased soon after to 200 men and by 1490 to 600. Green and white (the Tudor colours) were worn from 1485 and no mention is made of the traditional red uniform until 1514. The gold garland and red rose were repeated on the back of the tunic. The Guard carried halberds but remained trained archers. It is possible that earlier guards wore the liveries of their respective kings: Edward I and II, white and red; Edward III, mauve and red; Richard II, white and green; Henry IV, V and VI, white and blue; Edward IV and Richard III, mauve and blue.

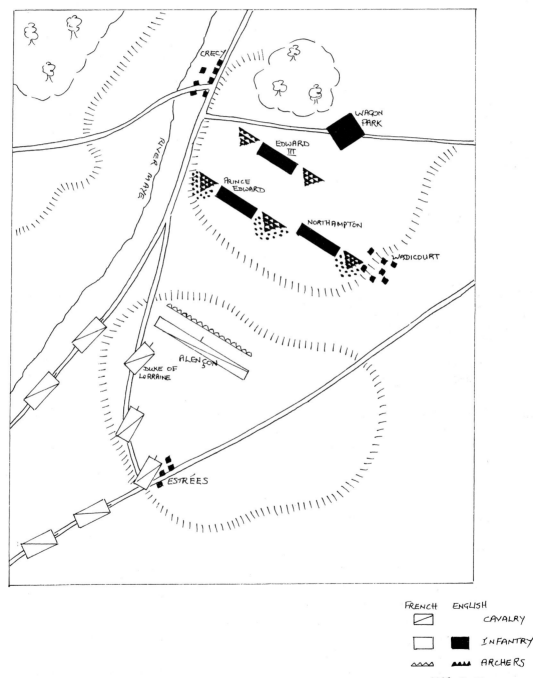

CRECY 1346 At Crecy Edward III drew up his forces in what was to become the standard order of battle used by English armies throughout the 100 Years War

H. *Flags.*

1 Bourbon standard
2 Standard of Edward III
3 Standard of Joan of Arc
4 Pavon pennoncelle of Reynald, Lord of Agincourt
5 Pennoncelle of the Clares, Earls of Gloucester
6 Pennoncelle of the Percy family of Northumberland
7 Pennon of the French Infantry, 1479
8 Banner of Uri Canton
9 Banner of the Treasurer of the Teutonic Order
10 Banner of the Teutonic Order
11 Banner of Brabant
12 Banner of Burgundy
13 Banner of Richard II and Henry V of England

FLAGS

The pennoncelle took three forms: pavon (Reynald), single tail (Clare), and swallow tail (Percy). The pavon shape was popular in the fourteenth century. These pennoncelles were carried at the lance head and were the personal flags of all men-at-arms from knight up. Length was twelve to eighteen inches, with the tails taking up half that length. The pennoncelle bore the arms of its owner, but in the fifteenth century it became customary to use a badge on a livery colour (as in the Percy pennoncelle) and this was known as a badge pennoncelle.

The pennon was a larger version of the pennon-celle, between two and three feet long. It was the personal flag of a knight bachelor and in the fifteenth century also had a badge form. If a knight was promoted to banneret on the battle-field the tails were cut off his pennon to produce a banner.

The banner was the flag of all ranks above knight banneret. It was never displayed unless the owner was present, and then only if battle was about to be joined. The banner of the four-teenth century was from two to three feet deep and twelve to eighteen inches wide, although a two- to three feet-square version became pre-dominant later. A badge form became popular in the late fifteenth century. The banner used by Henry V and Richard II incorporated the cross and martlets banner of Edward the Confessor, one of the five banners carried by English troops until 1485. The Treasurer of the Teutonic Order led the mercenaries at the battle of Tannenberg (1410).

The standard was granted to the nobility and knights banneret. It was not a personal flag but was used to mark the position of commanders' troops within an army. It was never furled during a campaign, being used to mark the group's H.Q. in camp, at the head of the force on the march, to lead attacks, and to provide a rallying point. It was from six to twelve feet long, depending on the rank of the owner.